4803 8490

★ IT'S MY STATE! ★

HAWAII

Ann Graham Gaines

Jacqueline Laks Gorman

Marshall Cavendish
Benchmark

New York

Published by Marshall Cavendish Benchmark
An imprint of Marshall Cavendish Corporation

Other Marshall Cavendish Offices:
Marshall Cavendish International (Asia) Private Limited, 1 New Industrial Road, Singapore 536196 •
Marshall Cavendish International (Thailand) Co Ltd. 253 Asoke, 12th Flr, Sukhumvit 21 Road, Klongtoey Nua,
Wattana, Bangkok 10110, Thailand • Marshall Cavendish (Malaysia) Sdn Bhd, Times Subang, Lot 46, Subang
Hi-Tech Industrial Park, Batu Tiga, 40000 Shah Alam, Selangor Darul Ehsan, Malaysia

Marshall Cavendish is a trademark of Times Publishing Limited

All websites were available and accurate when this book was sent to press.

Library of Congress Cataloging-in-Publication Data
Gaines, Ann.
        Hawaii / Ann Graham Gaines, Jacqueline Laks Gorman. — 2nd ed.
            p. cm. — (It's my state!)
        Includes bibliographical references and index.
        Summary: "Surveys the history, geography, government, economy, and people of Hawaii"—Provided by publisher.
        ISBN 978-1-60870-656-3 (print) — ISBN 978-1-60870-811-6 (ebook)
        1. Hawaii—Juvenile literature. I. Gorman, Jacqueline Laks, 1955- II. Title. III. Series.
    DU623.25.G35 2013
    996.9—dc23   2011020730

Second Edition developed for Marshall Cavendish Benchmark by RJF Publishing LLC (www.RJFpublishing.com)
Series Designer, Second Edition: Tammy West/Westgraphix LLC
Editor, Second Edition: Emily Dolbear

All maps, illustrations, and graphics © Marshall Cavendish Corporation. Maps and artwork on pages 6, 32, 33, 75, 76, and back cover by Christopher Santoro. Map and graphics on pages 10 and 43 by Westgraphix LLC.

The photographs in this book are used by permission and through the courtesy of:
Front cover: Carmel Studios/Superstock and Pacific Stock/Superstock (inset).
Alamy: Terry Smith Images, 4 (left); David L. Moore, 4 (right); Stephen Frink Collection, 5 (left); Photo Resource Hawaii, 5 (right), 20, 23 (left), 40, 45, 52 (top); 52 (bottom); Jacques Jangoux, 8; Douglas Peebles Photography, 11, 19; Rick Strange, 14; John Elk III, 15, 29; Lazlo Podor, 17; Dennis Frates, 18; WaterFrame, 23 (right); Mauro Ladu, 26; Classic Image, 28; North Wind Picture Archives, 35; Greg Vaughn, 36 (bottom); Debra Behr, 43; John Oeth, 46; Lonely Planet Images, 53; Ellen Isaacs, 54; David Moore—Oahu, 58; foodfolio, 65; Craig Ellenwood, 73. **Associated Press:** Karin Stanton, 16; Jim Collins, 22 (left); Jim Schultz, 23 (right); Associated Press, 34, 36 (top); Marco Garcia, 38; Jae C. Hong, 49 (top); Scott A. Miller, 49 (bottom). **Corbis:** Historical Collection, 30; Radius Images, 62; Specialist Stock, 66. **Getty Images:** National Geographic, 42; AFP, 57; Getty Images, 61; CBS, 74. **North Wind Picture Archives:** 24, 41, 48. **Superstock:** Science Faction, 12; Pacific Stock, 21, 27, 64, 67, 68; Alvis Upitis, 50; Flirt, 70; Ron Dahlquist, 71 (top); JTB Photo, 71 (bottom); age fotostock, 72.

Printed in Malaysia (T).
135642

CONTENTS

THE ALOHA STATE

State Bird: Nene

The nene (pronounced nay-nay), or Hawaiian goose, is a black and gray goose that lives only in Hawaii. Unlike all other geese, the nene does not live near water. Instead, most nene today live on the slopes of the Mauna Kea and Mauna Loa volcanoes, on the Big Island of Hawaii.

State Flower: Hibiscus

In 1988, Hawaii's state legislature declared the yellow hibiscus as the official state flower. Hibiscus flowers can come in a range of colors, including white, red, or pink. These striking flowers attract butterflies and hummingbirds.

State Tree: Kukui

The kukui, or candlenut tree, was brought to Hawaii by the first Polynesian settlers more than a thousand years ago. The tree's nuts, which are rich in oil, provided a source of light for the early Hawaiians. They placed the nuts in stone lamps and in torches and then lit them. They also used the kukui wood to build canoes and the tree's inner bark to dye cloth. The kukui was chosen as Hawaii's official state tree in 1959.

State Gem: Black Coral

Black coral are tiny marine animals that live in colonies (groups) in tropical oceans. When many of these small animals grow together, their colonies look almost like trees. Black coral can be found in shady, shallow water and deep in underwater caves. Early Hawaiians harvested the skeletons of black coral to use as charms and to make medicine. Today, black coral is often used in jewelry.

State Marine Mammal: Humpback Whale

Female humpback whales, which are generally larger than males, can grow to be about 45 feet (14 meters) long. Every winter, thousands of humpback whales migrate from the icy waters off Alaska to the warm oceans around the Hawaiian Islands. There, they breed, give birth, and care for their young. To help protect the whales, the federal government established the Hawaiian Islands Humpback Whale National Marine Sanctuary in 1992.

State Dance: Hula

Hula has been performed in Hawaii since Polynesian people first came to the islands. Hula dancers honored their Hawaiian gods and rulers with their dances. Today, there are two different types of hula. Traditional hula dances are performed to chanted poetry and are often accompanied with the sounds of drumming. Modern hula dances are performed to music from steel guitars, ukuleles, and drums.

HAWAII

N
W • E
S

NI'IHAU KAUA'I   O'AHU   MOLOKA'I MAUI
LANA'I KAHO'OLAWE
HAWAI'I

KAUA'I

NAPALI COAST STATE PARK
WAILUA RIVER
KAWAIKINI
Kapaa
WAIMEA CANYON
Kekaha Hanamaulu
Lihue
Kalaheo
WAILUA FALLS
HULEIA NATIONAL WILDLIFE REFUGE
BIRTHPLACE OF PRINCE KUHIO

NI'IHAU

KAULAKAHI CHANNEL

O'AHU

WAIMEA BAY
JAMES CAMPELL NATIONAL WILDLIFE REFUGE
La'ie
Hau'ula
WAIALUA BAY
Waialua
WAI'ANAE RANGE
KA'ALA
KAHANA VALLEY STATE PARK
KAMAILE'UNA RIDGE
Wahiawa
KANE'OHE BAY
PYRAMID ROCK
NU'UPIA POND
Makaha
Wai'anae
Ma'ili
Makakilo
Waipahu
Pearl City
Kane'ohe KAILUA BAY Waimanalo Beach
Kailua
KO'OLAU RANGE
Nanakuli
'Aiea
KE'EHI LAGOON
Ewa Beach
PEARL HARBOR
Waikiki
Honolulu
WAIKIKI BEACH
Diamond Head
KOKO HEAD REGIONAL PARK
HANAUMA BAY NATURE PRESERVE

Hawi
BIRTHPLACE OF KING KAMEHAMEHA
PU'UKOHOLA HEIAU NATIONAL HISTORIC SITE
KAWAIHAE BAY
HAPUNA BEACH STATE RECREATION AREA
KIHOLO BAY
POLOLU VALLEY
KOHALA MOUNTAINS
WAIMEA
MAUNA KEA
Laupahoehoe
AKAKA FALLS STATE PARK
Hilo HILO BAY
Kailua Kona
MAUNA KEA STATE RECREATION AREA
MAUNA LOA
Captain Cook
Mountain View
LAVA TREE STATE MONUMENT
KILAUEA CRATER
HAWAII VOLCANOES NATIONAL PARK

HAWAI'I

THE LABELS ON THIS MAP REFLECT THE OFFICIAL HAWAIIAN NAMES OF THE ISLANDS AND SITES

PUNALU'U BEACH PARK
GREEN SAND BEACH

MAUNA LOA
KAUPAPA PENINSULA
CAPE HALAWA
Kaunakakai

MOLOKA'I

Wailuku Kahului
Lahaina
PINEAPPLE
LANAIHALE
Lanai City
LANA'I
KEALAKAHIKI CHANNEL
ALALAKEIKI CHANNEL
LUAMAKIKI
PU'U'ULA'ULA
POLIPOLI SPRING STATE RECREATION AREA
HALEAKALA NATIONAL PARK
WAI'ANAPANAPA STATE PARK
WAILUA FALLS
POOLS OF 'OHE'O

MAUI

KAHO'OLAWE

★ 1 ★
The Aloha State

The state of Hawaii is located in the middle of the Pacific Ocean. The state is north of the equator. Hawaii is made up of an archipelago, or chain of islands. Because it is surrounded by so much water, the Hawaiian archipelago is the most isolated population center on Earth.

California lies about 2,390 miles (3,850 kilometers) to the east of Hawaii, while Japan is almost 4,000 miles (6,400 km) to the west. In the past, it took weeks to reach Hawaii in a sailing ship. Today, it takes travelers from California less than six hours to get to Hawaii by airplane. Many people consider Hawaii a paradise because of its remote location and its incredible natural beauty.

A Chain of Islands

If you look at most maps of the state of Hawaii, you will see only eight islands. In fact, the state covers the entire Hawaiian archipelago, which includes 132 islands, reefs, and shoals (sandy elevations), many of which are tiny, with areas of less than 50 acres (20 hectares). Although Hawaii is far from being the world's largest archipelago, it is still quite long. The Hawaiian archipelago stretches over a distance of more than 1,500 miles (2,400 km). In terms of land area, Hawaii is made up of only 6,423 square miles (16,635 square kilometers), which makes

Quick Facts

HAWAII BORDERS
Hawaii is completely surrounded by the Pacific Ocean.

The Napali Coast is a stretch of mountains on Kauai's northwest shore. Breathtaking cliffs tower over the sea.

it one of the smallest states. But the state also includes another 4,500 square miles (11,650 sq km) of water—found in the islands' many bays and inlets, and in some of the surrounding ocean waters.

Hawaii's eight main islands are clustered at the southeastern end of the Hawaiian archipelago. They spread out over a distance of 350 miles (565 km). Going from the southeast to the northwest, they are Hawaii (also called the Big Island), Maui, Kahoolawe, Lanai, Molokai, Oahu, Kauai, and Niihau. People live on just seven of these eight islands since Kahoolawe is now abandoned. During and after World War II (1939–1945), the U.S. Navy used Kahoolawe to practice bombing exercises. Although this practice ended in 1990, the island still has no permanent residents. Kahoolawe is currently being cleaned and restored. By state law, it can be used only for limited purposes, including native Hawaiian cultural and spiritual endeavors and historic preservation.

The state of Hawaii has four governmental counties—Hawaii, Honolulu, Kauai, and Maui. There is also a fifth county, called Kalawao, run by the state department of health. Kalawao is on the island of Molokai.

In the early days, to get from one island to another, Hawaiians traveled by canoe. Today, most people travel from one island to another by airplane, helicopter, or boat.

HAWAII

MAUI

MAUI

KALAWAO

MAUI

MAUI

HONOLULU

KAUAI

KAUAI

Hawaii has 5 counties.

Volcanic Origins

The Hawaiian Islands are actually the tops of volcanoes. The bottoms of these volcanoes sit on the ocean floor. The land that lies above the waves is considered an island.

According to geologists (scientists who study Earth's structure and history), Earth's surface is broken up into huge pieces called plates. These plates move slowly. Over the years, they bump together, causing earthquakes. Hawaii sits in the middle of a plate in the Pacific Ocean. Many millions of years ago, this Pacific Plate began to slowly pass over what is called a hot spot. At the hot spot, magma—hot, melted rock—bubbled up through Earth's crust and formed the Hawaiian volcanoes, one by one. (When magma reaches the surface, it is called lava.) Slowly, each of the volcanoes moved off the hot spot, and over time the volcanoes formed a long chain.

The oldest volcanoes, located at the northern end of the chain, have now sunk entirely beneath the waves. Others have sunk but not all the way. They are now just reefs, with only the tops of the volcanoes still visible. Others, like the active volcano Kilauea on the Big Island, remain high above the water. (The reason the Big Island has active volcanoes is because it is still over the hot spot.) The newest of the Hawaiian volcanoes— Loihi, which is located about

Kilauea, on the Big Island, is said to be the world's most active volcano.

Mauna Loa, in Hawaii Volcanoes National Park, last erupted in 1984.

20 miles (30 km) southeast of the Big Island—has not yet reached the ocean's surface.

In Hawaii, four volcanoes have erupted in the past two hundred years. Today, thousands of visitors go to see all four volcanoes each year. Three of the volcanoes—Mauna Loa, Kilauea, and Hualalai—are on the Big Island. Haleakala, which is in Haleakala National Park, is on Maui. Haleakala is the world's largest dormant, or inactive, volcano. Mauna Loa, which last erupted in 1984, is the world's largest active volcano. Kilauea was erupting for most of the nineteenth century, and it has erupted more than thirty times since 1952.

Quick Facts

UNDERWATER VOLCANO
The volcano Loihi, which is still underwater, keeps actively erupting. Scientists think that it could form a new Hawaiian island in ten thousand years.

Since 1983, there has been an area on Kilauea where the lava flow is active. Hualalai, which last erupted in 1801, is considered a dormant volcano.

The Hawaiian Islands

Each of Hawaii's main islands is different. The island of Hawaii is the biggest—just over 4,000 square miles (10,400 sq km) in area—which is how it got its nickname of the Big Island. Formed by five volcanoes, the Big Island still has two active volcanoes: Mauna Loa and Kilauea. On the northern and southeastern coasts of the Big Island are high cliffs, with waterfalls that flow into the ocean. The Big Island has the second-largest population of any of the islands, with about 185,000 people. Still, it does not seem crowded because the people are spread out.

Maui, formed by two volcanoes, has many canyons on its mountainsides. There is an isthmus (a narrow strip of land that connects the two volcanoes) where the soil is rich and sugarcane grows easily. Maui is home to one of the world's largest banyan trees—it covers a city block—and home to the

RECORD HOLDER

Hawaii is a record holder among the states. Ka Lae, a point on the south side of the island of Hawaii, is the southernmost point in the United States. Thanks to its many islands and shoals, Hawaii is the widest state. Hawaii is not, however, the westernmost point in the United States. Alaska stretches farther out into the Pacific Ocean.

Iao Needle, a monolith (or mass of lava) that rises 1,200 feet (365 m) from the valley floor in Iao Valley State Park. Maui has a population of more than 154,000. Residents live in a few large towns and "upcountry," or out in a rural area where there are small villages.

The unpopulated island of Kahoolawe lies next to Maui. Until 1990, the U.S. Navy tested bombs there. The bombing left the island barren and dry. Efforts are now underway to clean up the island and reintroduce native plants.

For hundreds of years, the small and relatively wild island of Molokai was populated, like the other major islands in the chain. But in the 1860s, most of the healthy residents left after a leper colony was established there by the Hawaiian legislature and King Kamehameha V. Lepers are people who suffer from leprosy— now called Hansen's disease—a contagious disease that causes serious skin lesions and damage to the nerves, muscles, and eyes. Today, the island is home to a population of around eight thousand people, including a small group who still live in the

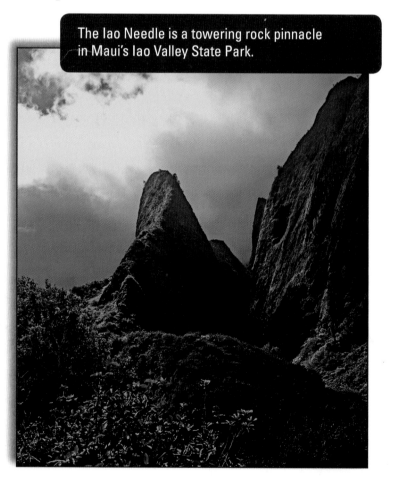

The Iao Needle is a towering rock pinnacle in Maui's Iao Valley State Park.

Kauai's Waimea Canyon has been called the "Grand Canyon of the Pacific."

former leper colony. Molokai attracts fewer tourists than the other islands of Hawaii.

The small island of Lanai, which measures just 18 miles (30 km) in length and 13 miles (20 km) in width, was once covered almost entirely by pineapple plantations. Now, it is home to luxury resorts. Like Molokai, Lanai has a small population, with about three thousand residents.

Oahu is the most populated island. There are a few stretches of wild coastline left on the island, but in other places it is almost entirely filled with businesses and homes. Oahu is known for its world-famous Waikiki Beach, a white-sand beach lined with resorts and hotels. The state's capital city of Honolulu, located on Oahu, is considered one of the world's most exotic cities. It has both beautiful tropical landscapes and modern high-rise buildings.

Kauai is known for its amazing Waimea Canyon. This canyon, lined with exotic vegetation, is 10 miles (16 km) long. The canyon was formed by rivers and floodwaters flowing down Mount Waialeale, which is one of the wettest places on Earth. Many famous movies, including *Jurassic Park*, have been

Quick Facts

SPECIAL TIME ZONES
The United States is divided into different time zones. Most of the zones cover many states. Hawaii and Alaska each has its own time zone, however.

filmed on Kauai. The island has a population of roughly 60,000 people, who live mostly in the island's small towns located along the coasts.

Niihau is privately owned. Only the owners, their workers, and their guests see this island. Niihau has a population of 250 people, almost all of whom are of Polynesian descent. Hawaiian is the main language spoken in most homes there.

The black sand found on some Hawaiian beaches contains tiny fragments of lava.

A Natural Paradise

Even though some cities are filled with modern buildings and crowds, the Hawaiian Islands still remain a place of astounding natural beauty. Surrounded by deep blue seas, the islands have beautiful beaches. In some places, the sand on these beaches is white and sparkling. Other beaches are made of black sand, formed when molten lava from a volcano poured into the ocean, cooled, and eventually wore down into sand particles. Other portions of Hawaii's coastlines offer dramatically high cliffs.

Hawaii's volcanic mountains all lie inland, and most of them are covered in thick tropical growth. Guava bushes, ferns, mango trees, and many more plants grow along the slopes.

Hawaii is home to several spectacularly different and fragile ecosystems. Ecosystems are natural areas in which living organisms—plants and animals—interact. A rain forest is an example of an ecosystem. On Mauna Loa, there is a rain forest where the jungle is thick and full of birds. On one side of Mauna Kea, on the other hand, there is a different, dry forest. Little rain falls on the area, which is perfect for plants such as silversword—a rare, low-growing plant with clusters of pointed leaves and tall purple or red flowers—and for other desertlike plants, such as cacti.

The Hakalau Forest National Wildlife Refuge on the Big Island protects ohia and koa trees, which are large and can reach heights of up to 80 feet (24 m). Especially interesting is the terrain around Kilauea, where lava flows often destroy the plants. Despite this, tiny new plants manage to push up through the lava and grow. The Big Island is also home to the lush Waipio Valley.

Other interesting features in Hawaii include the black volcanic rock found on the islands, as well as Molokai's and Kauai's unique red soil. This volcanic soil has a relatively high iron content.

Quick Facts

THE WORLD'S TALLEST MOUNTAIN

Mauna Kea is the tallest mountain in the world. Measured from its base at the ocean floor to its tip, it has an elevation of about 18,000 feet (5,500 m) below sea level and another 13,796 feet (4,205 m) above sea level. The total elevation is well over 31,000 feet (9,450 m), much taller than Asia's Mount Everest, which is about 29,000 feet (8,840 m).

Silversword is a rare plant that grows on the side of Mauna Kea.

The Olo'upena Falls, on Molokai, are surrounded by huge mountains.

Although there are no large rivers or lakes in Hawaii, there are many beautiful small rivers and estuaries, the aquatic habitats at the mouths of rivers. The Wailuku River, which starts on the slopes of Mauna Kea on the Big Island, is the state's longest river. Kauai has several rivers, too. They are popular with kayakers.

Hawaii is also the location of some of the world's most spectacular waterfalls. Olo'upena Falls on Molokai is the fourth-tallest waterfall in the world. But many of Hawaii's waterfalls are hidden and hard to reach. Another interesting natural water phenomenon is the blowhole, where ocean water spouts up through lava tubes.

Hawaii's Climate

Hawaii has only two true seasons: summer (called *Kau* in Hawaiian), which runs from May to October, and winter (called *Hooilo*), which runs from November to April. Many people find Hawaii's climate ideal. Although it can be humid, trade winds usually bring cool air off the ocean, and temperatures are consistent throughout the year. The average daytime summer temperature at sea level is 85 degrees Fahrenheit (29 degrees Celsius).

Quick Facts

NICE AND WARM
Hawaii is the only state where there has never been a recorded temperature below 0 °F (−18 °C). The coldest temperature ever recorded in the state was 12 °F (−11 °C) at Mauna Kea in 1979.

The average daytime winter temperature is 78 °F (25 °C). The highest temperature ever recorded in Hawaii was 100 °F (38 °C). That record was set in 1931 at Pahala on the Big Island. Temperatures can be cold high up in the mountains.

Each island has a windward side and a leeward side. The windward side is reached first by the prevailing winds blowing in off the Pacific Ocean, and it tends to be cooler and to get more rain. The leeward side is more protected from the winds off the ocean water, and it tends to be sunnier, warmer, and drier.

During the winter, snow sometimes falls on the Big Island at the top of Mauna Kea and Mauna Loa.

Rainfall varies greatly over the islands. On the island of Hawaii, the small port of Kawaihae, located on the northwestern shore, typically gets only 8 or 9 inches (20 or 23 centimeters) of rain per year. But the city of Hilo, located on the eastern shore of the Big Island, gets an average of 130 inches (330 cm) per year. On Kauai, Mount Waialeale—one of the wettest places on Earth—averages more than 460 inches (1,170 cm) of rain per year.

The forces of nature can be strong in Hawaii. There have been many volcanic eruptions, earthquakes, hurricanes, flash floods, and even occasional, disastrous tsunamis. A tsunami is a series of huge waves following an undersea disturbance such as an earthquake. Hilo was hit by tsunamis in 1946 and 1960.

Hawaii's Plant Life

When many people think of trees in Hawaii, palm trees often come to mind. But Hawaii has many other kinds of trees. One of these is the ohia, a very tall tree covered with red, yellow, or orange lehua flowers, that grows on volcanic slopes.

The koa tree can grow up to 100 feet (30 m) tall. People in Hawaii are trying to encourage new growth of these trees.

The hard red wood of the koa tree was used to make canoes in earlier times and is used to make furniture today. Other native trees include the guava and the banyan.

Plants that Hawaiians grow for food include sugarcane, pineapple, papaya, banana, mango, guava, lichee, avocado, breadfruit, macadamia nut, lime, passion fruit, and tamarind. There are also many different flowers that bloom all over Hawaii. These include orchids, anthuriums, and plumeria.

Animals in Hawaii

Before humans came, the hoary bat and the monk seal were the only mammals native to Hawaii. There were also many kinds of native lizards, insects, and birds. Offshore, a variety of fish, including marlin, dolphin, and tuna, swam in the waters. Today, hundreds of species of fish live in Hawaiian waters.

UNIQUE PLANTS AND ANIMALS

The islands of Hawaii are located thousands of miles from any other piece of land. The islands were never connected to any landmass. So how did plants and animals get there? The seeds of some plants came to Hawaii by air, carried by birds or the wind. Other seeds came by water, drifting across the ocean. Different types of fish and other animals swam to the islands, and birds flew there—sometimes after being blown off course by a storm. Since the islands were so isolated for so long, different species developed in new ways. Many of today's plants and animals are found only in Hawaii.

When the islands' first inhabitants arrived more than a thousand years ago, they brought with them dogs and pigs. They also brought rats, which had hidden in their boats and canoes. Later, Europeans brought cats, horses, cattle, goats, and sheep. In 1883, the mongoose, a catlike meat-eating mammal, was introduced to Hawaii. Farmers hoped it would eat the rats ruining their sugarcane crops. The mongooses ate some rats but not enough to solve the problem.

Because of loss of habitat, pollution, and other changes to the land and water, many species in the Hawaiian Islands are endangered, or in danger of completely dying out. Hawaiians are working to keep these species from disappearing forever. They are aware how important wildlife is to their islands.

SAVING THE NENE
In the late 1700s, 25,000 nene (Hawaiian geese) lived on the islands of Hawaii, Maui, and Kauai. But by the 1940s, only fifty nene were left. They had been killed by hunters and predators and suffered from habitat loss. A special recovery program was set up during the 1970s at Hawaii Volcanoes National Park. Today, although the nene is still endangered, there are approximately nine hundred in the wild and up to two thousand in breeding programs and zoos.

Hundreds of pygmy killer whales live several miles off the Hawaiian Islands, but they are rarely seen.

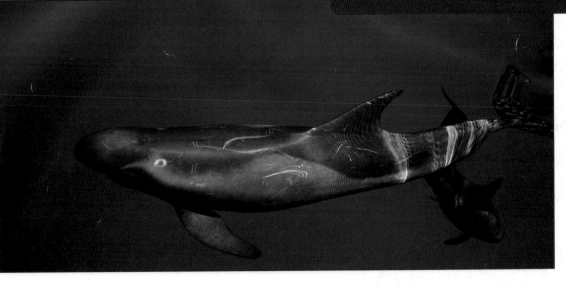

Hawaiian Monk Seal

Hawaiian monk seals are one of only two mammals native to Hawaii. Measuring up to 8 feet (2.4 m) in length and weighing up to 600 pounds (270 kilograms), monk seals are less social than other seals. In the ocean, monk seals dive deep—as much as 500 feet (150 m) below the surface—to catch reef fish, lobsters, and octopuses. Today, only about one thousand monk seals live on and off the Hawaiian Islands. They are endangered, in part from harm caused by discarded fishing nets.

Green Sea Turtle

When baby green sea turtles hatch, their shells are only about 2 inches (5 cm) long. By the time they have grown up, their shells can be more than 2 feet (60 cm) long. Adult turtles may weigh more than 400 pounds (180 kg). Scientists believe that some green sea turtles can live up to eighty years or more.

Hawaiian Hoary Bat

Hawaiian hoary bats are forest dwellers that hunt over open land. Unlike most bats, which live in colonies, they roost or make their homes alone. These bats are endangered, and scientists fear that they may soon become extinct, or die out. But because the hoary bat is hard to catch or observe, scientists are not sure how many remain.

Ohia Tree

The ohia is a tree found on many of the islands of Hawaii. Ohia trees produce an attractive red flower called the lehua. A Hawaiian myth says that there was once a warrior named Ohia. The goddess Pele fell in love with him, but he was already in love with a beautiful girl named Lehua. Pele was so angry that she turned him into a tree. Other gods turned Lehua into a flower on the tree so that Ohia and Lehua could always be together.

Honeycreeper

Many different kinds of honeycreeper birds live in Hawaii. A number of them are endangered. Honeycreepers live in forests high on the mountains. The most interesting-looking honeycreepers are brightly colored and have curved bills. These bills help them drink nectar out of flowers. The iiwi, for example, is a brilliant red honeycreeper with a hooked bill. The iiwi lives in forests of ohia trees and feeds off the trees' flowers.

Triggerfish

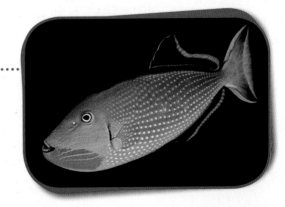

Hawaiian waters—especially the coral reefs around the islands—are home to many different fish, including the triggerfish. Different types of triggerfish have distinctive markings or colors. The humuhumunukunuku apua'a, or humuhumu for short, is Hawaii's state fish.

2

From the Beginning

Hawaii was one of the last places on Earth to be settled by humans. Scientists believe Polynesians—people from islands in the central and southern Pacific Ocean—first arrived in Hawaii sometime between 300 CE and 750 CE.

For years, Polynesians traveled to and from the different islands in the Pacific Ocean. To get to many of these islands, they built huge seagoing canoes. Each canoe was big enough to hold dozens of people and to travel hundreds or even thousands of miles. Because there were no maps and no landmarks in the middle of the ocean, travelers had to depend on natural signs to tell them where they were. These signs included ocean swells, currents, winds, and cloud formations. At night, they read the stars to find their way.

Experts believe that Polynesian travelers—probably from the Marquesas, which are islands in the southern Pacific Ocean—set out to find a new place to settle. These settlers might have been the first to arrive in the Hawaiian Islands. A second wave of settlement in Hawaii occurred around 1000 to 1300. These new people probably came from Tahiti.

Most of what is known of ancient Hawaiian history comes from stories told by the Hawaiian people. This form of storytelling is called oral tradition. Stories and myths have been passed down from one generation to the next. Archaeologists (scientists who study the artifacts, or remains, of ancient people)

For the Hawaiian people, much of daily life traditionally revolved around the islands' coastal waters.

HAWAII'S NAME

Historians disagree about the origin of Hawaii's name. Some believe the islands were named after a fisherman named Hawaii Loa. Others think the name comes from *Hawaiki*, a native word for "homeland," which was the name Polynesians used for the island they originally came from.

face challenges trying to add information because weather and time have destroyed most of the islands' ancient buildings and artifacts.

The Early Way of Life

Kings, chiefs, and priests ruled each individual Hawaiian island one thousand years ago, but the islands were not united into a single kingdom. Chiefs claimed large plots of land as well as areas along the coast. They gave smaller portions of land to the rest of the people to farm. Most people had to grow enough food to give an annual tribute to their chief as well as feed their families.

Religion was important to the early natives. Ancient Hawaiians worshiped Ku, the god of war. Many of the Hawaiians' other gods were of nature. Children grew up hearing legends of Pele, the goddess of volcanoes, whom Hawaiians believed demanded human sacrifice. Public worship took place in a temple called a heiau. Inside the heiau there was an altar, a raised platform, and carved images.

Traditional Hawaiian statues stand at Pu'uhonua o Honaunau National Historical Park on the Big Island.

The arts were important to the ancient Hawaiians. They used wood, shell, stone, and bone in carvings and jewelry. They developed elaborate calendars that told them when to plant certain crops. Athletic contests were frequently held. Ancient Hawaiians traveled by canoe to fish and to visit other islands, sometimes to trade and other times to fight.

Captain Cook

In 1778, the first European ships landed at Waimea on Kauai. British navy captain James Cook, one of the most important explorers of his day, was their commander. Hawaiian myth explained that one day the god Lono would come from the sea on a floating island. Many Hawaiians believed that Cook was this god.

Captain Cook judged his first visit to Hawaii as a great success. His crews greatly enjoyed the time they spent on the islands, which Cook named the Sandwich Islands. He described them as a tropical paradise. When he returned

Quick Facts

OUTRIGGER CANOES
For centuries, Hawaiians have built huge outrigger canoes capable of making long ocean voyages. Outrigger canoes have a main section where people sit, carved out of wood. Attached to the sides of the canoes are outriggers, or floats, that help balance the canoe.

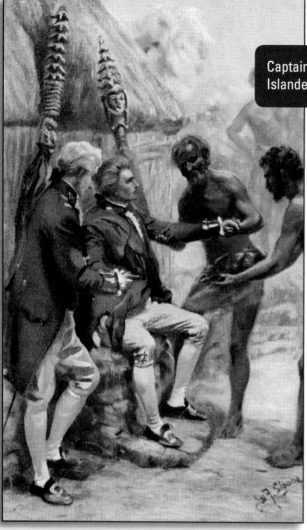

Captain James Cook was welcomed by Hawaiian Islanders when he arrived in 1778.

in 1779 for a second visit, however, trouble erupted. Cook and a few natives on the Big Island got into an argument over a boat that the British believed the natives had stolen. Cook was killed and his crew fled the islands on their ships.

Cook's death did not end European interest in the islands, however. The British wanted to establish trade with China. One thing the Chinese wanted was sandalwood, which grew in Hawaii. European and American traders came to Hawaii to look for the sweet-smelling sandalwood to sell in China for a great deal of money.

A New Kingdom

Around the time Captain Cook first visited the islands, a young warrior named Kamehameha lived in Kohala on the northern shores of the Big Island. He fought to rule the island, and by 1790, he controlled most of it. From there, he fought for control of the other islands. By 1810, having united all the islands into a single kingdom, he had become Hawaii's first king.

Kamehameha I welcomed people from other countries. He found them interesting and liked the goods they brought. Over time, Hawaiians became more and more accustomed to the foreigners. A few Hawaiians even agreed to leave Hawaii to travel to other lands. In Great Britain and the United States, these Hawaiians created a great stir. Missionaries—people who traveled to new places

A statue of King Kamehameha I stands in downtown Honolulu, in front of the building that houses the state supreme court.

In this historical engraving, a Christian missionary teaches Hawaiian Islanders about his religion.

to spread their religion—were interested in bringing their Christian beliefs to the islands and the people who lived there.

In 1819, two important things happened. First, King Kamehameha I died. He was succeeded by his son, Kamehameha II, who was advised by one of the late king's wives. Second, American whaling ships came for the first time. With the arrival of the whalers, Hawaii's ports began to develop. The whaling ships came back to Hawaii every winter.

In 1820, after voyages that lasted many months, missionaries arrived from New England. Over the years, fifteen different groups of missionaries came. The missionaries affected the lives of Hawaiian people in many ways. For instance, the missionaries forced Hawaiians to stop wearing their traditional clothing and

THE HAWAIIAN ALPHABET

The written Hawaiian alphabet developed by the missionaries contains only twelve letters: the vowels *a, e, i, o,* and *u* and the consonants *h, k, l, m, n, p,* and *w.* Two symbols—the okina (the ' mark) and the macron (a line placed over a letter)—are also parts of the alphabet.

dancing the hula. The missionaries also developed a written Hawaiian language and taught many native people to read and write.

Kamehameha's family remained in power for five generations. Under the influence of the missionaries, Kamehameha III developed a written constitution in 1840. He also passed the Great Mahele in 1848, which established a system of land ownership, letting people other than the king—including foreigners—own property.

Kamehameha III and his successor, Kamehameha IV, faced challenges from Europeans and Americans, however. For a long time, Great Britain, France, and the United States had all promised to allow Hawaii to remain independent. But all of these countries wanted to possess the islands, especially after Hawaii became a major producer and exporter of sugarcane. Many of the sugarcane plantations were owned by foreigners (often former missionary families), and as the years went on, cheap labor was brought in from other countries, such as China and Japan.

In 1872, Kamehameha V died. In the years that followed, there were struggles over the throne. In addition, U.S. influence became greater and greater. This was especially true after people such as Honolulu-born Sanford Dole established pineapple plantations on the islands. The business owners, including people from the United States, wanted a great deal of say in how the islands were run.

THE OLDEST SCHOOL

The missionaries brought European and American education to Hawaii. Maui's Lahainaluna is the oldest high school west of the Rockies. It was founded in 1831 by missionaries.

MAKING A TANGRAM PUZZLE

The fascinating puzzle called a tangram originated in China. Asian immigrants brought the puzzles with them to the Hawaiian Islands in the 1800s. Tangrams soon became popular with Hawaiians of all ages.

WHAT YOU NEED

1 sheet of stiff cardboard—at least 8 inches
   by 8 inches (20 cm by 20 cm)

Pencil

Ruler

Scissors

Newspaper

Paintbrush

Poster paint

To make the tans (shapes):

With a pencil and ruler, mark an 8-inch (20-cm) square on the cardboard. Cut out the square.

   Mark dots 2 inches (5 cm) apart along all four sides of the square. Connect the dots with light pencil lines to make a grid of sixteen squares.

   Using this diagram as a reference, mark the five cutting lines on the grid. Make these lines dark enough so that you can see where to cut. Cut along the five dark lines to create seven tans.

   Spread newspaper on your work surface and paint the tans. When they are dry, you are ready to play.

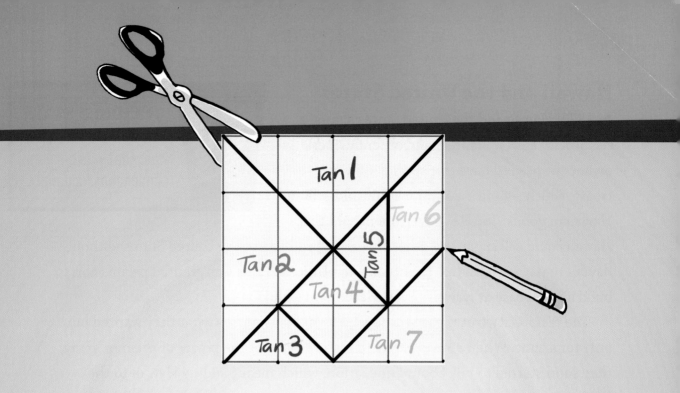

To play with the puzzle:

Arrange all seven pieces to make a shape—for example, a bunny or a sailboat. All seven tans must be used.

To turn the puzzle into a game, have two players take turns, each making a shape that has not yet been made. See who can make the most shapes.

Bunny

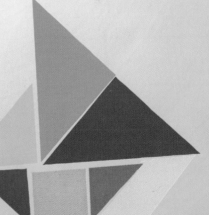

Sailboat

Hawaii and the United States

In 1875, Hawaii and the United States signed a reciprocity treaty. Planters and other business owners wanted to have this special kind of treaty, which set out rules for trading and selling Hawaiian goods. The U.S. government said that Hawaii could sell sugar and other Hawaiian products in the United States without having to pay an extra tax. Eventually, the United States was granted permission to build a naval base at Hawaii's Pearl Harbor, on Oahu.

Quick Facts

THE ONLY STATE
Hawaii is the only U.S. state that was once an independent monarchy.

The reciprocity treaty gave those who owned businesses what they wanted but only for a time. When efforts began to restore some of the power of the monarchy, they soon started to talk about annexation, which meant adding Hawaii to the United States.

Native Hawaiians did not want their land to become part of the United States. They preferred to remain free and independent. In 1893, after Hawaiian queen Liliuokalani introduced a new constitution, Americans living in Hawaii—led by Sanford Dole and acting on their own—overthrew her kingdom. They took away her power and started their own government in Hawaii.

Although U.S. president Grover Cleveland demanded that Hawaii be given back to its people, he refused to take any further action. Those who had taken over Hawaii ignored Cleveland's wishes and formed a republic in 1894, with Dole as president. The U.S. government officially recognized the republic.

In 1898, during the presidency of William McKinley, the Hawaiian Islands

Queen Liliuokalani was Hawaii's first queen and its last monarch. Her kingdom was overthrown in 1893.

Sanford Dole, shown at the center of the front row, became president when a republic was formed in Hawaii in 1894.

were annexed by the United States. Many native Hawaiians remained opposed, but the United States was too powerful. Leaders in the United States had come to consider Hawaii a necessity for defending the Pacific region. In 1900, the Hawaiian Islands were formally organized as a U.S. territory, with Sanford Dole as governor. (Throughout the history of the United States, new lands were often organized as territories before becoming states.)

The Twentieth Century

In the opening decades of the twentieth century, Hawaiians began to realize they could make money and help their economy by attracting tourists to the islands. A tourist committee was formed for the first time in 1903. In 1915, *The Aloha Guide*—the first guidebook devoted to Hawaii—was published. The first luxury passenger ship docked in Hawaii in 1927.

During the early years of the twentieth century, the islands attracted both tourists and new residents, and Hawaii's population grew rapidly. In 1900, the territory had a population of 154,001. By 1920, the number climbed to 255,881. In 1935, planes first carried mail across the Pacific, from California to the Philippines, with stops in Hawaii and other Pacific islands.

Growth of tourism was accompanied by the development of military bases in Hawaii. It is one of the only places in the middle of the Pacific Ocean where ships

The USS *Arizona* was one of the battleships destroyed when Japan attacked Pearl Harbor on December 7, 1941.

can safely dock for long periods of time. Its location is strategic. In the early 1900s, the U.S. Navy built an important naval base at Pearl Harbor, a sheltered bay on Oahu.

Pearl Harbor later played a meaningful role in World War II, which began in Europe in 1939. On December 7, 1941, Japanese bombers taking off from aircraft carriers attacked U.S. naval ships and planes located at Pearl Harbor and nearby air bases, killing some 2,400 Americans. The surprise attack forced the United States to enter World War II.

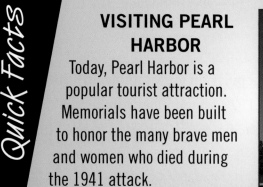

Quick Facts

VISITING PEARL HARBOR
Today, Pearl Harbor is a popular tourist attraction. Memorials have been built to honor the many brave men and women who died during the 1941 attack.

During the war, Japan was the enemy of the United States. Unfortunately, life became difficult for Japanese immigrants and Japanese Americans living on the U.S. mainland and in Hawaii. Even though most of them did not support Japan, they suffered from discrimination and poor treatment. Many of them were fired from their jobs or forced out of business. World War II ended in 1945, but it was a while before Japanese Americans were treated as equal members of society.

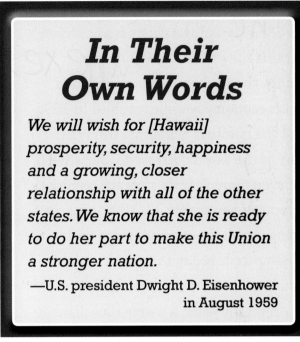

In Their Own Words

We will wish for [Hawaii] prosperity, security, happiness and a growing, closer relationship with all of the other states. We know that she is ready to do her part to make this Union a stronger nation.

—U.S. president Dwight D. Eisenhower in August 1959

Hawaiian Statehood

After the war was over, Hawaii headed toward statehood. In March 1959, the U.S. Congress passed an act making Hawaii a state, which President Dwight D. Eisenhower signed into law. Then, in June, Hawaiians voted on whether they wanted to become a state or not. They voted overwhelmingly in favor of statehood, 94 percent to 6 percent.

Finally, on August 21, 1959, Hawaii officially became the fiftieth U.S. state. Many Hawaiians celebrated the occasion. They would now receive full representation in the federal government. Their voices would be heard, and they would receive the same benefits from the U.S. government that people in all states receive.

Quick Facts

THE 49TH AND 50TH STATES
Alaska and Hawaii were both admitted to the United States in 1959. Alaska became the forty-ninth state in January. Hawaii did not join until August. As a result, the United States flag had forty-nine stars for only a few months.

In the 1960s and the following decades, Hawaii saw changes as tourism became the state's major industry. Things changed again, however, when Asia's economy became troubled in 1995 and the numbers of visitors from that part of the world decreased. Tourism fell off even more sharply after the terrorist attacks of September 11, 2001, because many travelers preferred not to fly. When people began to travel in greater numbers, tourists returned to Hawaii.

In recent years, a native Hawaiian independence movement has become active. Different groups believe that the islands were illegally seized in 1893, when Queen Liliuokalani and her monarchy were overthrown. In 1993, the U.S. Congress passed a resolution called the Apology Bill apologizing to native Hawaiians for the overthrow and the participation of U.S. citizens and "agents."

The Office of Hawaiian Affairs, a state agency, has been charged with representing the interests of native Hawaiians since 1978. In addition, the U.S. Congress continues to consider a bill to give federal recognition to the special status of native Hawaiians.

> ## In Their Own Words
>
> *[Native Hawaiians] are part of the diverse people of Hawaii who, as children of pioneers and immigrants from around the world, carry on the unique cultures and traditions of their forebears. As Americans, we can all admire these traits, as well as the raw natural beauty of the islands themselves.*
>
> —U.S. president Barack Obama, declaring King Kamehameha Day on June 10, 2010

Some native Hawaiians today are seeking Hawaiian independence.

★ **300 CE–750 CE** The first Polynesians arrive in Hawaii.

★ **1000–1300** A second wave of settlers comes from Polynesia (probably Tahiti).

★ **1778** Captain James Cook and the crews of his ships arrive at the islands. He is killed the following year.

★ **1810** King Kamehameha I unifies the islands under his kingdom.

★ **1819** Whaling ships arrive in Hawaii.

★ **1820** American missionaries arrive.

★ **1840** Hawaiians write their first constitution.

★ **1848** Under the Great Mahele, commoners are allowed to own land.

★ **1875** The kingdom of Hawaii enters into a reciprocity treaty with the United States.

★ **1893** Queen Liliuokalani is overthrown by Americans living in Hawaii.

★ **1894** The Republic of Hawaii is established.

★ **1898** The United States annexes Hawaii.

★ **1900** Hawaii is formally organized as a U.S. territory.

★ **1941** On December 7, Japanese warplanes attack Pearl Harbor, bringing the United States into World War II.

★ **1959** On August 21, Hawaii becomes a state.

★ **1978** The state's constitution sets up an Office of Hawaiian Affairs to provide help for native Hawaiians.

★ **1993** The U.S. Congress passes a resolution apologizing for the participation of Americans in the 1893 overthrow of the kingdom.

★ **2002** Linda Lingle takes office as Hawaii's first female governor.

★ **2006** President George W. Bush establishes the Northwestern Hawaiian Islands Marine National Monument.

★ **2008** Barack Obama is elected president of the United States. He becomes the country's first African-American president and first president born in Hawaii.

The People

Based on its population, Hawaii is ranked fortieth among the fifty states. According to the 2010 U.S. Census, there were 1,360,301 people living in Hawaii as of April 1 of that year. Most Hawaiians—more than 950,000—live in Honolulu County.

People from Many Lands

Before Captain Cook came to the islands in 1778, the only people who lived in Hawaii were of Polynesian descent. After Cook died the following year and traders started to visit, a few Europeans came to live on the islands.

In the late 1780s, trading ships sailed to Hawaii with crews that included many Chinese sailors. Some of them jumped ship, preferring to live in what looked like paradise than on the seas. More and more Chinese people came over the years, especially between 1850 and 1898.

The first U.S. missionaries arrived in 1820. In the years that followed, the population of Americans living in

Honolulu was a busy port during the 1870s. It served as the center of commerce for the islands.

Young hula dancers perform the popular dance, keeping old Hawaiian traditions alive.

Hawaii grew steadily. In addition to missionaries, businesspeople, merchants, and craftspeople came to the islands.

In the mid–1800s, people from the mainland United States acquired land in Hawaii and developed sugarcane and pineapple plantations. Large numbers of Asians, including Chinese, Japanese, and Filipinos (people from the Philippines), came to work in the fields. The lives of these people were extremely hard. Many worked for cruel bosses for almost no money. Nevertheless, many of these people remained in Hawaii. Some men sent for their relatives, while others married Hawaiian women.

A Different Type of State

Today, Hawaii differs from the other forty-nine states because there is no ethnic majority. In other words, no single ethnic group makes up more than half of the population.

The largest group is of Asian descent. Asian Americans make up more than 38 percent of the population. Caucasians—or white people—make up almost one-quarter of the population. Native Hawaiians and people from other Pacific islands make up 10 percent of the population. The Hispanic population now also makes up almost 9 percent of the people of Hawaii. Many

Many Hawaiians are of mixed heritage. This man and his granddaughter are Filipino-Hawaiian.

Who Hawaiians Are

American Indian and Alaska Native
4,164 (0.3%)

Some Other Race
16,985 (1.2%)

Black or African American
21,424 (1.6%)

Native Hawaiian and Other Pacific Islander
135,422 (10.0%)

Two or More Races
320,629 (23.6%)

Asian
525,078 (38.6%)

White
336,559 (24.7%)

Total Population
1,360,301

Hispanics or Latinos:
- 120,842 people
- 8.9% of the state's population

Hispanics or Latinos may be of any race.

Note: The pie chart shows the racial breakdown of the state's population based on the categories used by the U.S. Bureau of the Census. The Census Bureau reports information for Hispanics or Latinos separately, since they may be of any race. Percentages in the pie chart may not add to 100 because of rounding.

Source: U.S. Bureau of the Census, 2010 Census

Quick Facts

HAWAIIAN COWBOYS

There have long been cowboys in Hawaii. British explorer George Vancouver brought a small herd of eight cattle to the islands in the 1790s. Eventually, the herd grew into large numbers of wild cattle, and King Kamehameha III hired three Mexican cowboys to handle the animals. There are now cowboys and ranches across the main islands. In fact, one of the biggest cattle ranches in the United States, called Parker Ranch, can be found on the Big Island.

Hispanic people living in Hawaii came to the state from Puerto Rico or are of Puerto Rican descent. Only 1.6 percent of the people who live in Hawaii are African American. Less than 1 percent (0.3 percent) is American Indian. With all of this diversity, it is no surprise that many Hawaiians are of mixed heritage. More than 23 percent of Hawaiians are descended from two or more races.

Many Hawaiian residents are from other states. Some Americans come to enjoy the tropical weather all year long. Others move to Hawaii to retire or start island-related businesses.

Culture and Traditions

One especially interesting thing about visiting Hawaii is seeing the many Polynesian influences. Although not many native Hawaiians—people who are directly descended from the first residents—are left in the area, many of their ways, and other island traditions, remain alive.

Many people on the islands like to wear loose-fitting, brightly colored clothing. Hawaiian shirts (also called aloha shirts), which are usually brightly colored and decorated with bright designs, are popular. Women also occasionally wear muumuus, which are long dresses decorated with flowers or patterns. During festivals and other celebrations, many Hawaiian women wear traditional clothing, such as grass skirts.

Poi is made from the cooked and pounded root of the taro plant.

The diet of Hawaiian residents resembles the diet of other Americans in many ways. But Hawaiians tend to eat more fruit because it is so plentiful on the islands. Many of the state's residents also eat traditional food such as poi. Poi is a dish made from the cooked and pounded root of the taro plant, which grows on the islands. To celebrate birthdays and other special occasions, many people in Hawaii hold feasts called luaus, which often feature a roasted pig.

Other elements of traditional Hawaiian culture include music and dance. Hawaiian music features instruments such as the ukulele and the slack-key guitar, which is tuned to produce unique sounds. There are also different types of drums made of gourds, sharkskin, coconuts, and other natural materials. As for dance, hula performances entertain residents and visitors and also honor the state's native history.

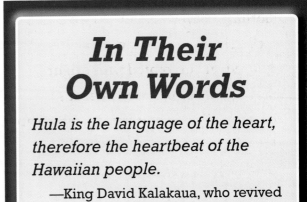

In Their Own Words

Hula is the language of the heart, therefore the heartbeat of the Hawaiian people.

—King David Kalakaua, who revived hula in the late nineteenth century

The Hawaiian language is also still alive. Some people speak the language fluently. In addition, those people who do not speak Hawaiian still know many words in this language. Many people use the word *aloha* as a greeting and call tourists *malihini*, a word that means "newcomer." Other Hawaiian words are *kai* (the sea), *mahalo* (thank you), *mauna* (mountain), and *ohana* (family).

Asian Influence

Hawaii is home to many people of Asian descent. Asian immigrants brought to Hawaii their own customs, languages, and religions. In Honolulu, there is a large Chinatown. The area has never been limited to Chinese people, however. Chinese, Vietnamese, Laotian,

Honolulu's Chinatown has shops and restaurants representing Chinese, Japanese, Thai, and other Asian cultures.

Japanese, Thai, Filipino, and Korean people all have shops and restaurants there. People come to the markets to buy special Asian products and foods. These specialty items include rice noodles and duck eggs.

Since the late twentieth century, historians have been collecting information about the history of Asian people in Hawaii. They have been trying to document, for example, the hard life that many Asian workers led on the islands' pineapple and sugarcane plantations.

Oral history projects collect people's stories, such as that of Japanese-born Tsuru Yamauchi, who moved to Hawaii in 1910 when she was twenty to join her husband, who already worked on a plantation. She explained her work on the plantation to an interviewer: "We moved to #10 Camp. I cooked and washed clothes there. . . . At that time we had to wash everything by hand, scoop and carry the water from the faucet to the bathhouse. . . . Oh, I sure did everything. And as for ironing, it was charcoal iron. We put in two pieces of charcoal and adjusted the heat until it got warm. I got paid one dollar a month per person. I did cooking, washing, everything. I got only one dollar. That is all."

In Their Own Words

Hawaii, Hawaii

Like a dream

So I came

But my tears

Are flowing now

In the canefields.

—Japanese folk song describing plantation life in Hawaii, called a *hole hole bushi* (*bushi* is Japanese for "songs" and *hole hole* is what Hawaiians called stripping leaves from dried sugarcane)

Quick Facts

SUMO WRESTLING

Sumo wrestling is a traditional Japanese sport common in Hawaii. In 1993, Hawaiian Chad Rowan became the first non-Japanese sumo wrestler to be named *yokzuna* (grand champion), which is the highest honor in the sport. He took the name Akebono when he began wrestling professionally.

Liliuokalani: Queen

Queen Liliuokalani was born as Lydia Kamakaeha in Honolulu in 1838. She became queen after the death of her brother, King David Kalakaua, in 1891. Two years later, Americans living in Hawaii overthrew her kingdom. She was forced to give up her claim to the throne. Afterward, she made a number of trips to the United States to protest the annexation of Hawaii. Queen Liliuokalani died in 1917. She is remembered as an accomplished songwriter and author, as well as a defender of Hawaiian traditions.

Father Damien: Missionary

Born in 1840 in Belgium, Joseph de Veuster adopted the name Father Damien when he traveled to Honolulu and became a priest in the 1860s. In 1873, Father Damien went to Molokai to minister to the hundreds of lepers who had been sent there to live in isolation. Father Damien improved their lives in many ways. He helped them to plant trees and build a water system and houses. He eventually contracted Hansen's disease and died on Molokai in 1889. The Roman Catholic Church made Father Damien a saint in 2009.

James Dole: Business Owner

James Drummond Dole, born in Massachusetts in 1877, was the first business owner to make a fortune selling pineapples. Arriving in Hawaii in 1899, he established his first pineapple plantation on Oahu. In the 1920s, he bought the entire island of Lanai to raise pineapples. Dole, who became known as the Pineapple King, died in 1958. The original Dole cannery closed in 1991, but Hawaiian farms that grow fruit for the Dole Food Company are still thriving.

Barack Obama: U.S. President

Barack H. Obama was born in Honolulu in 1961 to a mother from Kansas and a father from Kenya. He spent most of his early years in Hawaii. For college, he went to New York City to attend Columbia University. After graduation, Obama moved to Chicago to work with local community organizations. He earned a law degree at Harvard University and returned to Chicago, where he worked for a law firm and taught law. Obama was elected to the Illinois state senate in 1996 and to the U.S. Senate in 2004. In 2008, he was elected the forty-fourth president of the United States.

Laird Hamilton: Surfer

Laird Hamilton was born Laird Zerfas in San Francisco, California, in 1964. He moved to Hawaii with his mother when he was a baby. When he was a child, his mother married the famous surfer John Hamilton. By the time he was a teenager, Laird had also become a superb surfer. He is known today as the greatest and most innovative "big wave" surfer in the world, riding waves as tall as 70 feet (20 m) high.

Michelle Wie: Athlete

Born in Honolulu in 1989 to Korean-born parents, Michelle Wie began playing golf at the age of four. By ten, she was the youngest person ever to qualify for a United States Golf Association (USGA) amateur championship. In 2003, Wie became the youngest person to win a USGA adult event. Wie, who turned professional just before her sixteenth birthday, has played against both men and women. Her first professional Ladies Professional Golf Association (LPGA) tournament win was in 2009 and her second in 2010. When her schedule allows, she attends Stanford University in California.

Honolulu is Hawaii's largest city, as well as its capital.

Life in the Big City

Hawaii has just one very large city—its capital. The city of Honolulu, on Oahu, has a population of about 337,000. According to the 2010 Census, more than 950,000 Hawaiians live in or around Honolulu. That is about 70 percent of the state's population.

Honolulu is a city of contrasts, with tropical beaches, picturesque historic buildings, and gleaming, modern high-rise buildings. Many businesses are based in Honolulu, providing jobs for its citizens. Honolulu attracts many tourists, whose money helps the local economy. The city has beautiful parks and beaches. Many Honolulu residents complain about the city's traffic congestion and air and water pollution, however.

Life Away from the Big City

Hawaii's other cities are all much smaller. They include Pearl City, Hilo, Kailua, Kaneohe, Waipahu, Kahului, and Kailua-Kona.

On Oahu, Pearl City has a population of more than 47,000, growing more than 50 percent since the 2000 Census. Also on Oahu is Kaneohe, with more than 34,000 residents, and Waipahu, with about 38,000 residents. Hilo, on the eastern shores of the Big Island, has approximately 43,000 residents. Kahului on Maui has approximately 26,000 people.

Kailua-Kona, on the sunny side of the Big Island, has almost 12,000 residents. There are still many Hawaiians who live in small villages with little more than a school, a church, a small grocery store, and a post office. In many of these places, people live in old Hawaii-style frame houses with tin roofs.

People who live on Oahu enjoy many of the attractions of big cities. They shop at malls and go to museums, concerts, and theaters. While the other islands are also modern, their cities are not as crowded. Many feel that life on the less-populated islands moves at a slower pace.

Education

Missionaries founded the first schools in Hawaii in the 1820s. Then, about twenty years later, King Kamehameha III established a public school system.

Today, Hawaii's school system is unique among the states because it is one statewide system instead of a collection of different school systems run by individual local governments. In 2010, more than 178,000 students attended kindergarten through twelfth grade in 257 regular public schools and thirty-one charter schools. (Approximately 38,000 students attended private schools in the state.)

The University of Hawaii system has ten campuses on six islands, including seven community colleges. Almost 58,000 students are enrolled in this educational system. The largest and oldest school in the system is the University of Hawaii at Manoa, located on Oahu. Students there can study for undergraduate, graduate, and professional degrees.

★ Narcissus Festival

Held in Honolulu in January and February, the Narcissus Festival is part of the Hawaiian Chinese community's New Year celebrations. The festival, first held in 1950, includes the crowning of the Narcissus Queen.

★ Whale Day Celebration

Humpbacks are celebrated at Kalama Park, on Maui, one Saturday every February. People go there to learn about the whales as well as to eat, drink, buy arts and crafts, and take part in games and a parade.

★ Prince Kuhio Day

March 26 marks Prince Kuhio Day, a Hawaiian state holiday. It honors Prince Jonah Kuhio Kalanianaole, who served the Hawaiian territory as its delegate to the U.S. Congress from 1903 to 1922. Celebrations, including parades, luaus, canoe races, and festivals, are held throughout the state.

★ Merrie Monarch Festival

For almost fifty years, the Hawaii Island Chamber of Commerce has sponsored the Merrie Monarch Festival on the Big Island in April to preserve and promote traditional Hawaiian culture. The highlight is a three-day hula competition. Dancers prepare months in advance, taking lessons, attending seminars, and practicing.

★ Lei Day

On Lei Day, the first of May, many people in the Hawaiian Islands wear the traditional garlands of flowers or shells. There are celebrations throughout the state, including lei-making competitions and the crowning of a Lei Queen.

★ Celebration of Canoes

People come from many different Pacific nations to take part in Maui's annual celebration of canoes. At this May event, you can see canoes being carved or watch canoe races.

★ Pan Pacific Festival

When this festival began in 1980, people from Hawaii and Japan got together for many different kinds of cultural events. Now, at this June celebration, other cultures that contribute to Hawaii are also part of the fun, which includes music, art, theater, dance, and food.

★ Kamehameha Festival

This festival is held in June on King Kamehameha Day—Hawaii's oldest state holiday, honoring its first king. Held in Hilo on the Big Island, the festival pays tribute to Hawaiian culture with traditional dance, music, and arts and crafts.

★ Makawao Rodeo

Held on Maui, this is the largest rodeo held in Hawaii. This July event features *paniolo* (Hawaiian cowboys) taking part in traditional rodeo events. There is bull roping, bareback riding, rodeo clowns, and western music.

★ Ukulele Festival

Hundreds of the world's best ukulele players meet in July to play at the Ukulele Festival in Waikiki. There is even a ukulele orchestra made up of eight hundred musicians, most of them children.

★ Ironman Triathalon World Championship

Every October, athletes come from around the world to the Big Island to compete in this event. The difficult competition requires participants to swim 2.4 miles (3.8 km) in the ocean, bike for 112 miles (180 km), and run a 26.2-mile (42-km) marathon.

★ Kona Coffee Cultural Festival

The Kona Coffee Cultural Festival, held on the Big Island, lasts for two weeks in November. It includes many events celebrating not only Hawaii's coffee but also its growers.

How the Government Works

Like all other states, Hawaii is represented in the U.S. Congress in Washington, D.C. Each state has two senators in the U.S. Senate. A state's population determines the number of members it has in the U.S. House of Representatives. States with larger populations have more members. In 2011, Hawaii had two representatives.

Like other U.S. citizens, Hawaiians vote for president every four years. Hawaii also has a state government that works for everybody who lives on the islands.

County Government

In some ways, Hawaii's government is unlike that of any other state. At the local level, Hawaii has only county governments. Many other states have city and town governments in addition to county governments. County governments in Hawaii take on all the responsibilities usually held

Quick Facts

THE SIZE OF HONOLULU
Honolulu has the longest borders of any city or county in the world. The state constitution says that any island (or islet) belongs to Honolulu if it does not belong to another county. As a result, Honolulu is about 1,500 miles (2,400 km) long, or about as long as half the distance across the forty-eight states on the mainland.

The entrance to Hawaii's state capitol in Honolulu is lined with palm trees.

Branches of Government

EXECUTIVE ★ ★ ★ ★ ★ ★ ★ ★ ★

The executive branch enforces state laws. This branch includes the governor, lieutenant governor, attorney general, and state agencies, such as the department of health and the department of budget and finance. The governor and lieutenant governor are elected to four-year terms. The governor and lieutenant governor can serve only two terms. The governor appoints the attorney general.

LEGISLATIVE ★ ★ ★ ★ ★ ★ ★ ★

The legislative branch makes state laws. Hawaii's legislature is made up of two chambers, or parts—the state senate and the state house of representatives. The senate has twenty-five members. The house of representatives has fifty-one members. Members of the senate are elected to four-year terms. Members of the house of representatives are elected to two-year terms. There is no limit to how many terms a state legislator can serve.

JUDICIAL ★ ★ ★ ★ ★ ★ ★ ★ ★

Hawaii's supreme court is the highest court in the state. The justices on the supreme court can review state laws to determine whether they agree with or contradict the state constitution. The court has a chief justice and four associate justices. They are nominated by the governor and voted on by the state senate. The second-highest court is the intermediate court of appeals, which is made up of six judges. When a case is decided in a lower court but is appealed, it is this court that reviews the case to see if it was handled fairly and without error. Decisions by the intermediate court of appeals can be further appealed to the state supreme court. Like many states, Hawaii also has district courts, trial courts, family courts, and other lower-level courts.

by city or town governments in other states. For example, county governments are in charge of fire and emergency medical services, police forces, trash pickup, and street maintenance.

Today, Hawaii has four governmental counties. (A fifth county, called Kalawao County, is run by the state health department.) Some counties include more than one island. In Hawaii, it is the counties rather than cities that have a mayor.

State Government

Honolulu is Hawaii's state capital. Most of the state government's offices are located there.

Because Hawaii is such a new state, it has not had many governors. When Linda Lingle became governor of Hawaii in 2002, she became only the sixth elected governor in the state's history. She was also the first woman to be governor of Hawaii. Lingle was reelected in 2006. In Hawaii, the governor can serve only two terms, so Lingle was unable to run again in 2010. That year, Neil Abercrombie won election as the state's new governor.

Neil Abercrombie was elected governor of Hawaii in 2010. Before holding this position, he represented Hawaii in the U.S. House of Representatives for almost twenty years.

Iolani Palace in Honolulu was built in 1882. It has been designated a National Historic Landmark by the U.S. government.

In the past, the governor of the state lived in Queen Liliuokalani's mansion, called Washington Place. In 2002, a new building called the Governor's Residence was completed on the same grounds, and the mansion was turned into a museum. Visitors can also tour Iolani Palace, another former home of Queen Liliuokalani. After the overthrow of her monarchy in 1893, this building served as Hawaii's government headquarters until 1969.

Hawaii's state government has three branches—the executive, legislative, and judicial branches—which work to make laws and make sure that the laws are obeyed and interpreted correctly.

How a Bill Becomes a Law

It takes many steps for a bill to become a law in Hawaii. First, a state senator or member of the state house of representatives and his or her staff draft a bill and have it introduced in their chamber. The bill is assigned a number. After it is read, the bill is referred to a committee.

The committee holds hearings and can choose to change, pass, or reject the bill. A bill that makes it through committee is read for a second and third time in the senate or house, where members of that chamber can debate it.

Once the bill is passed by a majority vote of the members of the chamber where it was introduced, it is sent to the other chamber. There, it is debated and considered by a committee and voted on again.

If the second chamber passes the bill without

THE STATE CAPITOL
Hawaii has an unusual state capitol, which was opened in 1969. On the first floor are the chambers of the state senate and house of representatives, where the legislators meet. These chambers have walls that curve and slope, similar to cones, to symbolize volcanoes. The capitol also has an open courtyard in the middle, so that people inside the building can look up and see the Sun or stars.

changing it, it goes to the governor. But if the second chamber makes changes in the bill, a committee made up of members of both chambers must meet and produce a bill that both chambers can agree on. The final bill is read in both chambers and voted on. If it passes, the bill goes to the governor.

The governor can sign the bill into law or veto (reject) it. If the governor vetoes a bill, it can still become law if the house and senate overturn the governor's veto. In order to do this, two-thirds of both houses must vote to override the veto.

Getting Involved

Hawaiians have many opportunities to get involved in their government. Some people run for election and, if successful, hold public office. Others volunteer their time.

Many more citizens in Hawaii make their voices heard by contacting their legislators to tell them how they feel about an issue or how they want their legislators to vote on a specific bill. Anyone can call or write to their legislators' offices.

Many ideas for bills have actually come from Hawaiian residents. Over the years, residents of Hawaii have organized many times to bring about positive change. One thing they worked for was to stop the U.S. Navy from testing bombs on Kahoolawe. Hawaiians have also tried to get the government to protect the 'alala, or Hawaiian crow, and other species that are at risk. From local issues to state issues, everyone can make a difference.

DANIEL INOUYE

Daniel K. Inouye, the first Japanese American ever to serve in the U.S. Congress, has been a senator for Hawaii since 1963. Born and raised in Honolulu, Inouye is also a decorated war veteran who lost his right arm in battle during World War II. The highly respected senator has represented his home state in Washington, D.C., since 1959, when he became the state's first representative to the U.S. House of Representatives.

5

Making a Living

Long before explorers and missionaries came to the islands, Hawaiians had a subsistence economy. In other words, they did not make things to sell to other people. Families took care of themselves. They fished, grew crops, and made enough for what they needed. As time went on, different people began to specialize in different skills, such as building houses or boats or carving wood. Individuals also began to barter, or trade, with other people.

By 1800, ships were coming to Hawaii to trade. The people on the ships anchored off Lahaina, on the island of Maui, where they loaded their ships with sandalwood. American whalers began to sail every year to the north Pacific Ocean, hunting whales for their blubber. Whale blubber was processed into oil, which was used as fuel for lamps. On their way to the north Pacific, the captains of whaling ships often went to Hawaiian ports to pick up supplies and to allow their sailors to enjoy some time on the shore.

Americans and Europeans first bought land in Hawaii in order to grow sugarcane. Hawaii is an ideal place to raise sugarcane because the crop needs rich soil and much

Quick Facts

MACADAMIA NUTS
Smooth-shell macadamia trees were introduced to the islands in the 1880s. Hawaii is famous for the delicious nuts from these trees.

A Hawaiian resident of Laie, on Oahu, wears traditional clothes made of local items such as shells and feathers.

rain. Sugarcane is processed and made into sugar and other goods. Pineapple plantations were also set up to take advantage of the warm, wet weather.

Agriculture Today

For a long time, agriculture formed the backbone of the Hawaiian economy. This changed, however, in the twentieth century when Hawaiians began to make more money from tourism and the military.

Today, the state's largest ranches and plantations are almost all owned by corporations. There are many small farms, though. In 2009, there were 7,500 farms in Hawaii, with an average size of about 150 acres (60 ha). Sugarcane and pineapple are still important crops in Hawaii. Other important agricultural products are macadamia nuts, other fruits such as bananas and papayas, coffee, seed crops, vegetables including potatoes and cabbage, and flowers. Farms also raise beef cattle, dairy cows, hogs, and chickens (some raised for their meat and some for their eggs).

Rows of plants grow on a pineapple farm on Oahu.

RECIPE FOR COCONUT HAUPIA

In Hawaii, coconuts are used for a variety of foods and drinks. Follow these instructions to make this tasty coconut dessert. Haupia is often served at traditional luaus in Hawaii.

WHAT YOU NEED

12-ounce (355-milliliter) can of coconut milk (found in most grocery stores)

1 $\frac{1}{2}$ cups (355 ml) water

$\frac{1}{2}$ cup (120 grams) sugar

6 tablespoons (85 g) cornstarch

$\frac{1}{4}$ teaspoon (1.25 ml) vanilla

Have an adult help you with the stove. Mix the coconut milk and water together in a saucepan, and place the pan on the stove. Set the stove to low heat. Slowly add all the sugar, cornstarch, and vanilla to the pan. Keep stirring until the mixture thickens like a pudding. Be careful not to burn the mixture.

When it is thick, pour the haupia into an 8-inch by 8-inch (20-cm by 20-cm) pan and refrigerate.

When it is cool, the haupia will be firmer than regular pudding. You will be able to cut it into squares and serve it to your friends and family. Enjoy this tropical treat.

Tourists in Hawaii can take part in unusual activities such as swimming with dolphins.

Pacific Waters

Some Hawaiians make their living from the water. Many tourists love to fish in Hawaii, and the operators of charter boats earn money taking people out to fish in the Pacific Ocean. Snorkeling, surfing, and scuba diving are also popular sports. Instructors and stores that rent equipment to tourists can profit from Hawaii's waters.

A few thousand Hawaiians also make their living today catching fish. Ahi, also called bigeye tuna, and swordfish bring in the most money.

Today, there is also aquaculture around the islands. This involves growing animals and plants in the water. There are more than one hundred aquafarms in Hawaii. Some people involved in aquaculture raise algae, which are microscopic plants that fish and other small aquatic animals like to eat. Others raise shellfish such as shrimp, different kinds of finfish, and seaweed and other sea vegetables.

Tilapia are one type of fish being produced through aquaculture in Hawaii.

HOW THE UKULELE GOT ITS NAME

There are a number of theories about how the ukulele got its name. One story says the name means "jumping flea" and relates to the way the instrument is played. To play it, a person needs to move his or her fingers quickly up and down the strings. *Uku* in Hawaiian means "flea," and locals thought that the ukulele player's fast-moving fingers were like a flea jumping around.

Manufacturing

Manufacturing has never been an important part of Hawaii's economy. Besides food-processing plants, there are few factories. But manufacturing does provide a living for some Hawaiians.

Food-processing plants prepare and package food made from crops and animals grown on the islands. Printed materials, metal items, clothing, and textiles are among Hawaii's other manufactured products.

There are also some traditional goods that Hawaiians make and sell to other states or other countries. Hawaii is often associated with the ukulele. Portuguese immigrants who arrived in the late 1800s brought an early version of this little guitarlike instrument to the islands. Hawaiians grew to love the instrument and became skilled at playing and making ukuleles. There are several family-owned ukulele makers in Hawaii. Though factories in other states or countries make ukuleles, many musicians and collectors prefer to get their instruments from the Aloha State.

Workers & Industries

Industry	Number of People Working in That Industry	Percentage of All Workers Who Are Working in That Industry
Education and health care	127,309	21.0%
Publishing, media, entertainment, hotels, and restaurants	109,517	18.1%
Wholesale and retail businesses	85,063	14.0%
Professionals, scientists, and managers	63,550	10.5%
Government	47,757	7.9%
Construction	42,964	7.1%
Banking and finance, insurance, and real estate	42,132	6.9%
Transportation and public utilities	30,716	5.1%
Other services	26,875	4.4%
Manufacturing	22,232	3.7%
Farming, fishing, forestry, and mining	9,436	1.6%
Totals	**607,551**	**100%**

Notes: Figures above do not include people in the armed forces. "Professionals" includes people such as doctors and lawyers. Percentages may not add to 100 because of rounding.

Source: U.S. Bureau of the Census, 2009 estimates

Sugar

The first successful sugarcane plantation in Hawaii began operations on Kauai in 1835. Sugarcane is a tall grass plant that contains a sweet juice that is processed to become sucrose, or sugar. In 1959, when Hawaii became a state, one out of every twelve employed people in Hawaii worked in the sugar industry. That number has dropped over the years. By 2002, only about 2,500 Hawaiians worked directly or indirectly in the sugarcane industry. There are still sugarcane plantations in Hawaii, but the crop is not the moneymaker it once was.

Pineapple

The pineapple is a low-growing plant. It takes a long time to produce a fruit— more than a year after it is planted. Pineapples got their English name from their resemblance to pinecones. For decades, Hawaii had many pineapple plantations. Pineapples are no longer grown in huge numbers on the islands, but there are still thriving plantations. These farms employ a large number of Hawaiians, even though machines help harvest the fruit.

Cattle

Hawaii is home to many beef cows, which thrive on the islands' rich grasses. But ranchers have had trouble making much money from their beef, because they cannot afford to bring in grain for the cows to eat. The cost of shipping the cattle long distances to the mainland can also sometimes be a problem for ranchers. Still beef is an important state product.

Orchids

Orchids are showy and often sweet-smelling flowers. Hawaii's tropical climate is ideal for these plants. Many orchids grow wild in Hawaii's natural areas. But orchids are also specially grown on farms or in greenhouses to be sold to the rest of the United States, Europe, and Asia.

Military Bases

The federal government is a huge source of money for Hawaii because of the state's many military bases. The U.S. Navy first became interested in building a naval base at Pearl Harbor on Oahu in the 1800s, and in 1887, the United States received the exclusive right to use Pearl Harbor as a refueling and repair station for ships in the Pacific. Today, the U.S. Army, Air Force, and Marines also have bases in Hawaii. The government has also established satellite-tracking locations in the state. All of these military facilities provide jobs for Hawaii residents.

Coffee

Coffee is made from seeds (called "beans" after the outer covering is removed) that grow on evergreen trees. Farmers say it is the year-round warm weather, rich volcanic soil, and light winds and rain that make Hawaiian coffee special. Hawaii is the only U.S. state that grows coffee, and Kona is the most famous of all Hawaiian coffees.

Hawaii's dramatic scenery is one of the main attractions for tourists.

Tourism

Hawaii makes most of its money from tourism. In 2009, more than 6.4 million people visited Hawaii, and most stayed an average of nine days. Most visitors—about 70 percent—come from the United States, although Hawaii is also a popular destination for people from Asia. People travel to Hawaii mostly for pleasure, and many come to spend their honeymoons.

For many Americans, Hawaii is a memorable getaway where they can relax on tropical islands without leaving the country. The wildlife in Hawaii is unlike anywhere on the mainland. Many visitors hike through the forest, see the volcanoes, snorkel or scuba dive along the reefs, or simply relax on the beach. They also enjoy the various cultural events and historic sites.

Visitors who arrived in Hawaii by air spent $9.9 billion in 2009. Tourism helps Hawaii's income in many ways. Hotels, resorts, restaurants, museums, and stores where visitors spend their money employ many Hawaiians. And every time a new hotel is built to house more tourists, people in the construction industry are able to find new jobs.

Hawaii's Future

Today, Hawaii has economic problems that its leaders and citizens are trying to address. After the terrorist attacks of September 11, 2001, fewer tourists came to Hawaii, and businesses were hit hard. And when the economy of the United States—and that of the rest of the world—suffers, tourism to Hawaii slows down too. This is what happened beginning in late 2007. Economic downturns make it difficult for residents to find jobs. Some may decide to move to the mainland, where opportunities may be better.

Quick Facts

FOOTBALL IN HAWAII
Football bowl games have been played in Hawaii since the 1930s, when the Poi Bowl began. Since 2002, the Hawaii Bowl, now called the Sheraton Hawaii Bowl, has been played in December at Aloha Stadium in Honolulu. The Pro Bowl—an all-star game between National Football League players—was held at Aloha Stadium from 1980 to 2009. It returned there in January 2011.

It is expensive to live in Hawaii. Prices for many goods are always going to be high in Hawaii because they require ships or airplanes to transport them there. These goods include many foods and beverages.

There have been some positive changes in Hawaii's economy. For example, in recent years, there are more and more jobs in health care on the islands. The state is encouraging growth in science and technology, ocean research and development, health and education, tourism, different forms of agriculture, and floral and specialty food products that come only from Hawaii.

In addition, Hawaii is a popular location for film and television productions. The state is working to attract even more of these projects. Hawaii would also like to bring more sports events to the state. Hawaiians have had to deal with tough times before, and together, the state residents are committed to finding ways to keep the Aloha State's economy as prosperous as possible.

TELEVISION IN HAWAII

Hawaii has been called Hollywood's Tropical Backlot. It has the country's only state-operated film studio. Many TV shows have been shot in Hawaii. One recent show, *Lost*—which ran from 2004 to 2010—was filmed on Oahu. The crime show *Hawaii Five-O* had its debut in 1968 and ran until 1980. In the fall of 2010, a new version of *Hawaii Five-O* came out, featuring some of the same Hawaiian locations, along with the well-known song from the original show.

Hawaii's flag has the Union Jack—the flag of Great Britain—in its upper left-hand corner. The Union Jack appears because British explorer George Vancouver gave the British flag to King Kamehameha I as a gift. At the time, Kamehameha was bringing together the islands, and he decided to use the Union Jack as Hawaii's unofficial flag. Eventually, in 1816, eight red, white, and blue stripes were added to symbolize the eight main islands.

In the center of the seal is a design based on the old royal coat of arms of the Kingdom of Hawaii. King Kamehameha I is shown holding a staff, and the Goddess of Liberty is shown holding the Hawaiian flag. The seal also has many symbols including a tabu ball and stick, which stand for the power of the government. The seal also features eight taro leaves, a phoenix, and a star. The top of the seal has the words "State of Hawaii" and the year the state joined the union. The state's motto (which translates as "The life of land is perpetuated in righteousness") is on the bottom.

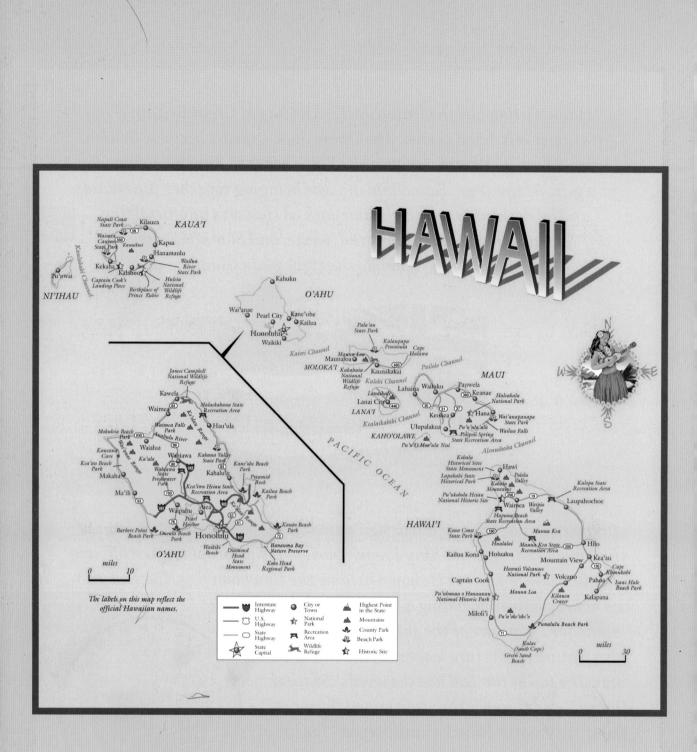

HAWAII

KAUA'I

Napali Coast State Park
Kilauea
Kapaa
Hanamaulu
Waimea Canyon State Park
Kawaikini
Kekaha
Kalaheo
Captain Cook's Landing Place
Birthplace of Prince Kuhio
Hulcia National Wildlife Refuge
Wailua River State Park

Kauiakahi Channel

Pu'uwai

NI'IHAU

Kahuku

O'AHU

Wai'anae
Pearl City
Kane'ohe
Kailua
Honolulu
Waikiki

Kaiwi Channel

Pala'au State Park
Kalaupapa Peninsula
Cape Halawa
Mauna Loa
Maunaloa
MOLOKA'I
Kaunakakai
Kakahaia National Wildlife Refuge
Kalohi Channel

Pailolo Channel

MAUI

Lahaina
Wailuku
Pauwela
Keanae
Haleakala National Park
Kahului
Lanaihale
LANA'I
Lanai City
Keokea
Hana
Wai'anapanapa State Park
Wailua Falls
Ulupalakua
Pu'u'ula'ula
Polipoli Spring State Recreation Area
Kealaikahiki Channel
KAHO'OLAWE
Pu'u'O-Moa'ula Nui
Alenuihaha Channel

James Campbell National Wildlife Refuge
Kawela
Waimea
Ko'olau Range
Malaekahana State Recreation Area
Waimea Falls Park
Hau'ula
Anahulu River
Mokuleia Beach Park
Waialua
Kaueana Cave
Wahiawa
Kahana Valley State Park
Kane'ohe Beach Park
Ka'ala
Kaneana Cave
Kea'au Beach Park
Wahiawa State Freshwater Park
Kahalu'u
Pyramid Rock
Makaha
Kea'iwa Heiau State Recreation Area
Kailua Beach Park
Ma'ili
Waipahu
Aiea
Ko'olau Range
Kaupo Beach Park
Pearl Harbor
Barbers Point Beach Park
Omenia Beach Park
Honolulu
Waikiki Beach
Diamond Head State Monument
Hanauma Bay Nature Preserve
Koko Head Regional Park

O'AHU

PACIFIC OCEAN

Kohala Historical Sites State Monument
Lapakahi State Historical Park
Hawi
Pololu Valley
Kohala Mountains
Pu'ukohola Heiau National Historic Site
Waimea
Waipio Valley
Kalopa State Recreation Area
Laupahoehoe
Hapuna Beach State Recreation Area
Kona Coast State Park
Mauna Kea
HAWAI'I
Hualalai
Mauna Kea State Recreation Area
Hilo
Kailua Kona
Holualoa
Mountain View
Kea'au
Captain Cook
Hawaii Volcanoes National Park
Volcano
Cape Kumukahi
Pahoa
Isaac Hale Beach Park
Pu'uhonua o Honaunau National Historic Park
Mauna Loa
Kilauea Crater
Kalapana
Miloli'i
Pu'u'oke'oke'o
Punalulu Beach Park
Kalae (South Cape) Green Sand Beach

miles 0 10

The labels on this map reflect the official Hawaiian names.

miles 0 30

Interstate Highway	City or Town	Highest Point in the State
U.S. Highway	National Park	Mountains
State Highway	Recreation Area	County Park
State Capital	Wildlife Refuge	Beach Park
		Historic Site

Hawaii Ponoi

words by King David Kalakaua
music by Henry Berger

BOOKS

Carolan, Dr., and Joanna Carolan. *A President from Hawaii*. Hanapepe, HI: Banana Patch Press, 2009.

Crowe, Ellie. *Hawaii: A Pictorial Celebration*. New York: Sterling Publishing, 2007.

Crowe, Ellie. *Kamehameha: The Boy Who Became a Warrior King*. Waipahu, HI: Island Heritage Publishing, 2008.

Feinstein, Stephen. *Hawai'i Volcanoes National Park: Adventure, Explore, Discover*. Berkeley Heights, NJ: MyReportLinks.com Books, 2009.

Mattern, Joanne. *Hawaii: Past and Present*. New York: Rosen Central, 2010.

Temple, Teri, and Bob Temple. *Welcome to Hawai'i Volcanoes National Park*. Chanhassen, MN: The Child's World, 2007.

WEBSITES

HawaiiHistory.org:
http://www.hawaiihistory.org

Hawaii's Official State Website:
http://www.ehawaii.gov

Hawaii's Official Tourism Site:
http://www.gohawaii.com

Hawai'i Volcanoes National Park:
http://www.nps.gov/havo

Ann Graham Gaines lives with her children deep in the woods of Texas. For close to twenty years, she has been writing children's nonfiction books and doing picture research. Every year she dreams of Hawaii: in January, when the icy winds blow off the plains, and in August, when the Texas heat seems like it will never end.

Jacqueline Laks Gorman has been a writer and editor for approximately thirty years. She was raised in New York and moved to the Midwest in the 1990s. She and her family live in DeKalb, Illinois, but they would love to visit Hawaii.

Page numbers in **boldface** are illustrations.